Creating and Selling
WORDPRESS
PLUGINS

Jamie Osborne

Creating and Selling Wordpress Plugins

Jamie Osborne

This book is for sale at http://leanpub.com/creatingandsellingwordpressplugins

This version was published on 2013-09-20

Contents

CONTENTS

Introduction

Welcome to Creating and Selling Wordpress Plugins. The following chapters will take you through the main steps you'll need to follow in order to create a working Wordpress plugin. Once created, we'll look into various ways of selling your plugin online.

Wordpress is an extremely popular platform. Some statistics indicate it runs on nearly 20% of all websites online! With such a large number of users working with the platform there is a very high demand for customized features, i.e. plugins. Learning how to create these plugins can lead to a healthy income online.

Creating a plugin doesn't have to be difficult and with this book you'll learn enough to create and sell your own Wordpress plugins.

Pre-requisites & Assumptions

This book is written with the assumption that the reader has at least a basic knowledge of web programming. That is, you understand the fundamentals of how websites are built. In our case that means using PHP, Javascript and SQL at a beginner to intermediate level. No advanced topics are covered in this book so even those with a passing knowledge of web programming should be able to pick up the concepts and put them to good use. As long as you are willing to supplement what's in this book with some other beginner books on web programming even a complete beginner can benefit.

Sample Code

All code samples in this book come from a complete working plugin created specifically for the purposes of teaching Wordpress plugin development concepts. The code samples highlight the main areas of importance and will give you a solid foundation for a Wordpress plugin. However, they are not a complete example on their own. You'll find the complete code is hosted on GitHub available to download at: https://github.com/josborne/creating-wordpress-plugins-sample-code[1]

---

[1] https://github.com/josborne/creating-wordpress-plugins-sample-code

Setting Up

It's recommended that you follow along writing code for each section in this book. If you already have a development environment setup you may skip this section. If not, we'll need to install a web server and Wordpress. When writing the book, a local Apache web server was used but you may use any web server you have available as long as it can support Wordpress. At the time of writing the minimum requirements for Wordpress (version 3.6) are PHP version 5.2.4+ and MySQL version 5.0+. You can find the latest information about minimum requirements here: http://wordpress.org/about/requirements/[2]

A quick and easy way to get a full distribution of the Apache web server, MySQL database and PHP is to use XAMPP from: http://www.apachefriends.org/en/xampp.html[3]

Once your web server is installed you'll want to download the self-hosted version of Wordpress from http://wordpress.org[4] and install it in your web server public folder. Installing Wordpress is straightforward, requiring you to create a database, update the *wp-config.php* with the database settings and then accessing Wordpress in a browser to run the install script. Full details can be found here: http://codex.wordpress.org/Installing_WordPress[5]

To write the code you can simply use Notepad. If you'd prefer a full development environment there are various free alternatives including https://netbeans.org/[6] and http://www.eclipse.org/[7]

---

[2]http://wordpress.org/about/requirements/

[3]http://www.apachefriends.org/en/xampp.html

[4]http://wordpress.org

[5]http://codex.wordpress.org/Installing_WordPress

[6]https://netbeans.org/

[7]http://www.eclipse.org/

Plugin Structure

There are various ways to structure your plugin files. For very small plugins you can simply create the main plugin file in *wp-content/plugins*. If you're creating a plugin with multiple files it is better to organize them into a directory structure like so:

/plugins

    /my-plugin

        /css

        /img

        /include

        /js

        /pages

        my-plugin.php

The main plugin file sits inside a folder with the same name located in *wp-content/plugins*. Our styles go in */css*, images in */img* and Javascript files in */js*. The */include* directory contains top level PHP code files we will include from our main plugin file. We will require access to things like database and other functions throughout all of the plugin code. Inside */pages* we place our PHP files that contain HTML markup for displaying, either as administrator or user-facing pages.

This is the structure we will be using throughout the following chapters of the book.

Creating the main plugin file

The main plugin file is the starting point for your plugin. Wordpress will run this file when a user activates the plugin. This is where you will create any definitions you require, include supporting plugin files and setup your plugin defaults.

The main plugin file should be the name of your plugin and located in the plugin folder: */wp-content/plugins/my-plugin/my-plugin.php*. We'll start out by creating a plugin header comment in *my-plugin.php* so that Wordpress will recognize it as a valid plugin.

```php
<?php
/*
Plugin Name: My Example Plugin
Plugin URI: http://example.com/my-plugin
Description: A plugin example from Creating Wordpress Plugins: A Step by Step
 Guide
Author: Jamie Osborne
Version: 1.0
Author URI: http://jamieos.com
*/
```

If you save that file and head to your Plugins menu in the administrator dashboard you should now see your new plugin listed as an available plugin to be activated. Activating it now won't do anything but at least it shows we're on the right track. If it doesn't appear in the list of plugins make sure you have placed the file in the correct location in your Wordpress installation and that you've followed the format of the header comment correctly.

Our next task is to create some definition constants. These constants are values we may need later on during development of our plugin so it's good practice to include them at the top of *my-plugin.php*.

```php
//defines
if ( !defined('MY_PLUGIN_NAME') )
    define('MY_PLUGIN_NAME', trim(dirname(plugin_basename(__FILE__)), '/'));
if ( !defined('MY_PLUGIN_PATH') )
    define ('MY_PLUGIN_PATH', WP_PLUGIN_URL . '/' . end(explode(
    DIRECTORY_SEPARATOR, dirname(__FILE__))));
if ( !defined('MY_PLUGIN_DIR') )
    define('MY_PLUGIN_DIR', WP_PLUGIN_DIR . '/' . MY_PLUGIN_NAME);
```

We start by defining the plugin name, in our case it will be 'my-plugin'. This uses the *plugin_-basename* Wordpress function which gets the path to the plugin, i.e. *my-plugin/my-plugin.php* and we strip the directory name from that, which will be the name of our plugin.

The plugin path and directory are useful constants, particularly for locating plugin supporting files like images, CSS, Javascript and so on. We will use these constants later on.

Next up, we'll include some of the plugin supporting files. For very small plugins, you can include all the code you need in your main plugin file but for anything larger it makes more sense to split the functionality into separate files. This way, each file is only responsible for its own piece of functionality. This makes it more readable and easier to make updates and fix errors. We will create these files later on.

```
//includes
include 'include/my-plugin-database.php';
include 'include/my-plugin-functions.php';
include 'include/my-plugin-admin.php';
```

A note about hooks

One of the key parts to understand when developing for Wordpress are hooks. A hook is a way you can attach a function to an action. Almost every action performed by Wordpress has a hook defined for it. In a usual Wordpress page request, Wordpress will go through each action in turn, such as printing the page title, loading the sidebar, placing links in the footer and so on. For each action, Wordpress also checks to see if any active plugins have hooks defined and if so, it will run those hooks as well. This is the main way that plugins interact with Wordpress to add custom features.

Here we will define some hooks which will be executed when your plugin is activated. These are called activation hooks and are created using the Wordpress function *register_activation_hook*.

```
//activation hooks
register_activation_hook(__FILE__, 'myplugin_setup_db');
if ( get_option('myplugin_options') == '' ) {
    register_activation_hook(__FILE__, 'myplugin_defaults');
}
function myplugin_defaults()
{
    $arr = array(
        'option1' => 'default1',
        'option2' => 'default2',
        'option3' => 'default3',
    );
    update_option('myplugin_options', $arr);
}
```

The first activation hook is attached to the function *myplugn_setup_db* which we will create later in the included *my-plugin-database.php* file. It will ensure the database is setup correctly when the user activates the plugin.

The second activation hook is tied to the myplugin_defaults function which you can see defined below. This ensures that there are some default values stored on activation of the plugin.

A note about options

Wordpress options are a simple way of saving plugin settings and user choices using the Wordpress functions *get_option* and *update_option*. We will go into more detail about options later on when creating the administrator menus.

Now that the main file has been created, we have a good starting point for our plugin development. It's time to move onto the next section, creating administrator menus.

Creating the administrator menus

Once the main file has been created, a good first step is to create the administrator menus for your plugin. Creating them early gives you a chance to think through all the possible options and features you want to offer and will make creating the plugin functionality easier later on.

The administrator menu (sometimes called settings menu) can be created in a variety of ways depending on how you'd like it to appear in the Wordpress dashboard. You can create a top-level or a sub-level style menu. The Wordpress documentation says that it's rare a plugin would need a top-level menu however this seems to be the favored style recently. The top-level menus sit at the same level as other Wordpress dashboard menus such as the Posts, Pages and Appearance and can contain a number of sub-menus. The sub-level menu will sit inside the top-level Settings menu as a sub-menu and will be just one page for your options.

Simple Menu

Our example plugin will create a top-level menu but here is how you can create a simple sub-menu inside the Settings menu.

```
add_action( 'admin_menu', 'my_plugin_menu' );
function my_plugin_menu() {
    add_options_page( 'My Plugin Settings, 'My Plugin', 'manage_options',
    'my-plugin-settings, 'my_plugin_settings_page' );
}
function my_plugin_settings_page () {
    if ( !current_user_can( 'manage_options' ) ) {
        wp_die( __(
        'You do not have sufficient permissions to access this page.'
        ) );
    }
    include MY_PLUGIN_DIR . '/pages/myplugin_simple_admin_page.php';
}
```

You would include this code in *my-plugin-admin.php* which is included from your main plugin file. The first line calls *add_action* which attaches the function '*my_plugin_menu*' to the Wordpress hook '*admin_menu*'. This means that *my_plugin_menu* will be called when Wordpress is creating the admin menus, effectively adding your menu as well. The *my_plugin_menu* function calls the Wordpress function *add_options_page* which creates the simple admin menu using the function *my_plugin_settings_page* (the last parameter) to output it. Finally, the *my_plugin_settings_page* function checks that the current user is authorized to view the page and if so, includes the PHP file which contains the page contents.

The steps involved in creating the menu page and dealing with user interaction and settings are the same for both the simple sub-menu and the top-level menu so that will be explained below.

Top-Level Menu

You can create a top-level administrator menu for larger plugins with lots of features and several settings pages. The following code in this section will go in *include/my-plugin-admin.php*. The first step is to setup the Wordpress hooks so that your menu will be created.

```
//Setup hooks and functions for admin menu
add_action('admin_init', 'myplugin_admin_init');
add_action('admin_menu', 'myplugin_menu_pages');
add_filter('plugin_action_links', 'myplugin_plugin_action_links', 10, 2);
```

Same as before, we use *add_action* to attach our own functions to the Wordpress hook actions. Here we're using *admin_init* which is called on initialization of the administrator menus, and *admin_-menu* which is triggered when Wordpress creates the menus. Lastly, we use *add_filter* to hook into the *plugin_action_links* Wordpress filter to add our own customizations. The *plugin_action_links* filter allows us to add our own menu option to the plugin list as seen on the top-level Plugins menu.

A note about filters

Wordpress filters are similar to actions in that they are ways you can attach your own functionality by 'hooking in' to parts of Wordpress execution. Filters are functions that Wordpress passes data through, at certain points in execution, just before taking some action with the data. Most input and output in Wordpress passes through some filter and you can add your own filtering by using the *add_filter* function with the appropriate filter.

Now we'll add the two functions we attached actions hooks to for initializing and creating the administrator menus.

```php
function myplugin_admin_init()
{
    wp_register_script('myplugin-js', MY_PLUGIN_PATH . '/js/myplugin-admin.js');
    wp_register_style('myplugin-css', MY_PLUGIN_PATH .
    '/css/myplugin-admin.css');
}
function myplugin_menu_pages()
{
    // Add the top-level admin menu
    $page_title = 'My Plugin Settings';
    $menu_title = 'My Plugin';
    $capability = 'manage_options';
    $menu_slug = 'myplugin-settings';
    $function = 'myplugin_settings';
    add_menu_page($page_title, $menu_title, $capability, $menu_slug, $function);

    // Add submenu page with same slug as parent to ensure no duplicates
    $sub_menu_title = 'Settings';
    $menu_hook = add_submenu_page($menu_slug, $page_title, $sub_menu_title,
        $capability, $menu_slug, $function);
    //this ensures script/styles only loaded for this plugin admin pages
    add_action('admin_print_scripts-' . $menu_hook, 'myplugin_admin_scripts');

    $submenu_page_title = 'My Plugin Page 1';
    $submenu_title = 'Page 1';
    $submenu_slug = 'myplugin-page1';
    $submenu_function = 'myplugin_page1';
    $menu_hook = add_submenu_page($menu_slug, $submenu_page_title,
        $submenu_title, $capability, $submenu_slug, $submenu_function);
    add_action('admin_print_scripts-' . $menu_hook, 'myplugin_admin_scripts');

    $submenu_page_title = 'My Plugin Page 2';
    $submenu_title = 'Page 2';
    $submenu_slug = 'myplugin-page2';
    $submenu_function = 'myplugin_page2';
    $menu_hook = add_submenu_page($menu_slug, $submenu_page_title,
        $submenu_title, $capability, $submenu_slug, $submenu_function);
    add_action('admin_print_scripts-' . $menu_hook, 'myplugin_admin_scripts');
}
```

There are a lot of new concepts in the above code so we'll go through it in more detail. Starting with *myplugin_admin_init* we are registering a script and a style with Wordpress. We will be using the style_ myplugin-admin.css_ to style the administrator menu pages and the script *myplugin-admin.js* will be used to save and submit any forms we may have using Ajax. More on those two files later.

The *myplugin_menu_pages* function is where we create the top-level menu plus two sub-menu pages. We first define the settings for the menu such as the name, title, capability, slug and function. The name and title are self-explanatory. The capability is for authorization purposes and set to '*manage_options*' which means the user must have permission to update settings in order to view this menu. There are many capabilities which are based upon the role assigned to the user. You can find the full list here: http://codex.wordpress.org/Roles_and_Capabilities[8]. The slug is the URL safe name you'll see in the browser bar when viewing this page and the function is the name of the function which will create this menu. We will define the functions later on. Once we have all the parameters defined we pass them to *add_menu_page* which instructs Wordpress to create a top-level menu item.

Next we create a sub-menu called 'Settings' which goes to the same page as when the top-level menu item is clicked. We use the same slug which tells Wordpress it is the same page. So now, when a user clicks on the top-level item 'My Plugin' or the sub-menu 'Settings' (which is below 'My Plugin') they will go to the settings page created by the *myplugin_settings* function.

You will notice that *add_submenu_page* returns a value which we're storing in *$menu_hook*. This is how we can attach functions to actions which are specific to that menu only. The *admin_print_-scripts* action is used to add scripts in-line to all of your administrator pages. However, if we append the *$menu_hook* returned from *add_submenu_page* to the *admin_print_scripts* action, we can add scripts to that one page only. This is useful if you wish to have different CSS or Javascript files for each menu page. You can see in the *add_action* function call we're appending the *$menu_hook* to the *admin_print_scripts* action with a dash '-' in between.

The following code shows two more sub-menu pages being created using *add_submenu_page* with different values for the name, title, slug and function parameters. We're also saving the *$menu_hook* for the same *admin_print_scripts* action as above.

Now we've defined how we want the menus setup, the next step is to create the functions we named earlier to create the pages and print the scripts.

```
function myplugin_admin_scripts()
{
    wp_enqueue_script('myplugin-js');
    wp_localize_script('myplugin-js', 'admin_ajaxurl',
        admin_url('admin-ajax.php'));
    wp_enqueue_style('myplugin-css');
}


function myplugin_settings()
{
```

---

[8]http://codex.wordpress.org/Roles_and_Capabilities

```php
    if ( !current_user_can('manage_options') ) {
        wp_die('You do not have sufficient permissions to access this page.');
    }
    include MY_PLUGIN_DIR . '/pages/myplugin_admin_page.php';
}

function myplugin_page1()
{
    if ( !current_user_can('manage_options') ) {
        wp_die('You do not have sufficient permissions to access this page.');
    }
    include MY_PLUGIN_DIR . '/pages/myplugin_admin_page_1.php';
}

function myplugin_page2()
{
    if ( !current_user_can('manage_options') ) {
        wp_die('You do not have sufficient permissions to access this page.');
    }
    include MY_PLUGIN_DIR . '/pages/myplugin_admin_page_2.php';
}
```

In *myplugin_admin_scripts* we enqueue the '*myplugin-js*' script that we registered earlier. This is the recommended way to include scripts into your plugin pages, rather than including '

The following functions simply check the user has permission to view the settings page and then include the page definitions using the *MY_PLUGIN_DIR _ constant to locate them correctly. Let's now take a look at the settings page, which we'll create in _pages/myplugin_admin_page.php.*

```php
<?php
$options = get_option('myplugin_options');
?>

<div class="wrap">
    <h2><?php echo __('My Plugin Settings', 'myplugin'); ?></h2>
    <div id="updateDiv"><p><strong id="updateMessage"></strong></p></div>
    <form action="" method="post" id="settings-form">
        <fieldset>
            <div id="legend">
                <legend class="legend">
                    <?php echo __('Update Settings', 'myplugin'); ?>
                    <img src="<?php echo MY_PLUGIN_PATH . '/img/loader.gif'; ?>"
                        alt="Loading..." class="showLoading"/>
```

```
                        </legend>
                    </div>
                    <p class="tips"></p>
                    <input type="hidden" name="action"
                            value="myplugin_update_settings"/>
                    <label for="option1"><?php _e("Option 1", 'myplugin'); ?> </label>
                    <input type="text" name="option1" id="option1"
                            value="<?php echo $options['option1']; ?>">

                    <label><?php _e("Option 2", 'myplugin'); ?> </label>
                    <label class="radio">
                        <input type="radio" name="option2" id="option2A" value="a"
                        <?php echo ($options['option2'] == 'a') ? 'checked' : '' ?> >
                        Choice A
                    </label>
                    <label class="radio">
                        <input type="radio" name="option2" id="option2B" value="b"
                        <?php echo ($options['option2'] == 'b') ? 'checked' : '' ?>>
                        Choice B
                    </label>

                    <label for="option3"><?php _e("Option 3", 'myplugin'); ?></label>
                    <select id="option3" name="option3">
                        <option value="usd" <?php echo
                        ($options['option3'] == 'usd') ? 'selected="selected"' : '' ?>>
                            United States Dollar</option>
                        <option value="cad" <?php echo
                        ($options['option3'] == 'cad') ? 'selected="selected"' : '' ?>>
                            Canadian Dollar</option>
                        <option value="gbp" <?php echo
                        ($options['option3'] == 'gbp') ? 'selected="selected"' : '' ?>>
                            British Pound</option>
                    </select>

                    <button type="submit" class="btn btn-success">
                        <?php esc_attr_e('Save Changes') ?></button>
                </fieldset>
            </form>
    </div>
```

myplugin_admin_page.php is where we're defining the settings page form so we can let our users choose various options we're providing with this plugin. Before we delve into this code, let's go over the flow of code which gets us to this point. In *my-plugin-admin.php* inside the *myplugin_-menu_pages* function we defined a sub-menu item called 'Settings' using *add_submenu_page*. The last parameter to *add_submenu_page* was the name of the function we want to use to show the page, which we called *myplugin_settings*. Now, *myplugin_settings* simply uses PHP include to add the contents of *myplugin_admin_page.php* whenever it is called i.e. when Wordpress wishes to show this menu due to user interaction (the user clicked on the 'Settings' menu item). It is at this point the contents of *myplugin_admin_page.php* are displayed.

Returning to the above *myplugin_admin_page.php* code we start out by retrieving the options so we can display them in the form. Next, we create a <div> with the *wrap* class. This is required for Wordpress to style the page correctly with the header and footer of standard administrator pages.

Now we define the form with three inputs; a text input, radio buttons and a drop down list. The form is quite standard HTML although you may notice that the form has no action and also the label text is outputted using the *_e* or *echo __* functions. The form has no action attribute because we will take care of form submission using our Javascript via Ajax. You'll see the hidden field "action" defines the value *myplugin_update_settings* which is how we link form submission to a PHP function to handle the inputs. We'll explain how this link is setup later. The *_e* and *echo ___ allow the label text to be translated if the user has a different language installed. These functions pass the text in the first parameter through the Wordpress _translate function to achieve this.*

The form inputs are set to the current option values. The radio buttons and drop down menu do this by adding the "checked" or "selected" attributes respectively based upon the option value.

Now that the form has been created we need a method of handling it when the form is submitted which includes saving the values each user enters. We will do this using Javascript with jQuery to capture the form submit event (when the user clicks the 'Save Changes' button) and post the form data back via Ajax to our PHP form handler code which will save the data. Let's take a look at the file *myplugin-admin.js*

```
jQuery(document).ready(function ($)
{
    $(".showLoading").hide();
    $("#updateDiv").hide();
    $('#settings-form').submit(function (e)
    {
        $(".showLoading").show();
        $(".tips").removeClass('alert alert-error');
        $(".tips").html("");

        var $form = $(this);

        // Disable the submit button
        $form.find('button').prop('disabled', true);
```

```
$.ajax({
    type:"POST",
    url:admin_ajaxurl,
    data:$form.serialize(),
    cache:false,
    dataType:"json",
    success:function (data)
    {
        $(".showLoading").hide();
        // re-enable the submit button
        $form.find('button').prop('disabled', false);
        if (data.success)
        {
            $("#updateMessage").text("Settings updated");
            $("#updateDiv").addClass('updated').show();
        }
        else
        {
            // show the errors on the form
            $(".tips").addClass('alert alert-error');
            $(".tips").html(data.msg);
            $(".tips").fadeIn(500).fadeOut(500).fadeIn(500);
        }
    }
});

return false;
    });
});
```

First, we hide the *showLoading* and *updateDiv* elements which are used to inform the user of the current UI state This is generally considered good practice when doing Ajax interactions. Next, we use a jQuery selector which is trigged when the form with the ID "*settings-form*" has the *submit* event. This happens when the user clicks the button with the *type="submit"* on the form in *myplugin_admin_page.php*. The next few lines show the loading image and clean up any error messages that may have been previously displayed. The form object is saved so we can use it to disable the submit button as well as use the jQuery *serialize* function. This encodes the form elements into a query string appropriate for submitting.

We use jQuery *$.ajax* to make the Ajax call to the *admin_ajaxurl* (we set this value earlier using *wp_localize_script*) passing the serialized form data. The *dataType* parameter is set to "*json*" because we'll pass back the result as a JSON object, which will be handled in the success function. The success function checks the JSON response from the server and if successful, adds the update message to the screen informing the user. If there was some kind of error, it is displayed to the user at the top of the form.

We can now submit the form via Ajax, so let's take a look at how to handle this form data on the server. The following code will go in our file, *my-plugin-functions.php*.

```php
add_action('wp_ajax_myplugin_update_settings', 'myplugin_update_settings');
function myplugin_update_settings()
{
    $option1 = $_POST['option1'];
    $option2= $_POST['option2'];
    $option3 = $_POST['option3'];

    // Save the options
    $options = get_option('myplugin_options');
    $options['option1'] = $option1;
    $options['option2'] = $option2;
    $options['option3'] = $option3;

    update_option('myplugin_options', $options);

    //the correct way to post JSON data back from Wordpress
    header("Content-Type: application/json");
    echo json_encode(array('success' => true));
    exit;
}
```

A note about Ajax hooks

We can use *wp_ajax* and *wp_ajax_nopriv* to hook into Wordpress using Ajax. In order for Wordpress to direct the Ajax request correctly, both of these hooks expect an action name appended to them as well. For example, *wp_ajax_my_action* would use the *wp_ajax* hook with the action called *my_-action*. Set the action name from the Javascript code by posting back a value named "action" as part of the Ajax request. The difference between *wp_ajax* and *wp_ajax_nopriv* is that *wp_ajax* only allows logged in users whereas *wp_ajax_nopriv* can be executed for users who are not logged in.

The first line of the above code sets our Ajax hook with the action *myplugin_update_settings* to run the function declared below it, also named *myplugin_update_settings*. If you take a look back at our settings form in *myplugin_admin_page.php* you will notice a hidden input named "*action*" with the value "*myplugin_update_settings*". This field gets sent as part of the Ajax call (part of the $form serialize) in our Javascript code so Wordpress knows what action we need. Now you can see how it all ties together. The form plus the action value is posted via Ajax in the Javascript and linked to a handler function on the server in *my-plugin-functions.php*.

The *myplugin_update_settings* function is quite straightforward. Firstly, it reads the PHP $*POST* *values from the form using the element name attributes and then updates the options using _update_-options.* Note, while out of the scope of this book, this is a great place to run some extra validation of the user input before saving it. At the very least you will want to verify the input is of the correct type and format and that it contains no malicious content.

Finally, we pass back the result to our Javascript Ajax function as a JSON object using the method suggested by Wordpress making sure to call *exit* at the end. If you do find any validation errors you could set `'success' => false` at this point to trigger the error display code shown earlier in the Javascript.

Summary

We have gone through the complete flow from defining administrator menu pages to handling the form input. The process is the same for adding additional menu pages. First, in *my-plugin-admin.php* add the sub-menu page using *add_submenu_page* and write the function which will include the page definition. Next, create the page making sure to create the page elements inside a <div> with the class "wrap" for proper styling. If the page contains a form, make sure to define an action and tie it to a *wp_ajax* or *wp_ajax_nopriv* hook and function in your *my-plugin-functions.php* file. Lastly, create the Javascript form submit handler to pass the serialized form to the server via Ajax.

Now we have our administrator menus in place, it's time to look at how to use the database through Wordpress.

Database

You can also create and use your own database tables for your plugin if storing and retrieving key value pairs using Wordpress options doesn't offer enough control. Wordpress defines a global variable *$wpdb* to allow developers access to database operations.

Back in the first section, you will remember we created an activation hook for setting up the database in our main plugin file, *my-plugin.php.*

```
register_activation_hook(__FILE__, 'myplugin_setup_db');
```

This calls *myplugin_setup_db* when the user activates this plugin. We'll create that function now in *include/my-plugin-database.php.*

```php
<?php
//required for dbDelta()
require_once(ABSPATH . 'wp-admin/includes/upgrade.php');
function myplugin_setup_db()
{
    global $wpdb;
    $table = $wpdb->prefix . 'myplugin_table';
    $sql = "CREATE TABLE " . $table . " (
        recordID INT NOT NULL AUTO_INCREMENT,
        title VARCHAR(100) NOT NULL,
        desc TEXT NOT NULL,
        isEnabled TINYINT(1),
        value INT NOT NULL,
        UNIQUE KEY recordID (recordID)
        );";

    //database write/update
    dbDelta($sql);
}
```

Before the function, we're including a Wordpress file that is not included by default in order to access the *dbDelta* function. The *dbDelta* function examines the current table structure, compares it to the desired table structure and either adds or modifies the table as necessary. It does have some specific requirements, like each field must be on its own line in the SQL statement and others. You can read all the requirements here: http://codex.wordpress.org/Creating_Tables_with_Plugins#Creating_or_Updating_the_Table[9].

---

[9]http://codex.wordpress.org/Creating_Tables_with_Plugins#Creating_or_Updating_the_Table

Inside *myplugin_setup_db* the first thing we do is get our global *$wpdb* so we can access the database. When creating the table name, notice how we prefix it with *$wpdb->prefix*? This is to ensure that the correct table prefix is used for the Wordpress tables. We can't assume the user has set 'wp_' as a prefix so we must check the value when creating tables.

Next is some basic SQL that creates a table with 6 columns of different types plus a primary key definition. All we need to do to run the SQL is pass the string to *dbDelta*. Now when a user activates this plugin this code will be run and (assuming the default prefix) a table called "wp_myplugin_table" will be created in their Wordpress database alongside the other Wordpress tables.

Let's define some functionality on the database tables now. I'll show the standard operations you may want to do on your new database table such as inserting records, updating records, deleting, and selecting.

```
function myplugin_insert_record($title, $desc, $isEnabled, $value)
{
    $data = array(
        'title' => $title,
        'desc' => $desc,
        'isEnabled' => $isEnabled,
        'value' => $value
    );

    global $wpdb;
    $rows_affected = $wpdb->insert($wpdb->prefix . 'myplugin_table', $data);
    if ( $rows_affected ) {
        return $wpdb->insert_id;
    } else return -1;
}
```

Here we are using the *$wpdb->insert* function to create a new row using the values passed into the function. These are then stored in an array indexed with the table column names. The *$wpdb->insert* function should return 1 if successful, *false* if not. Because we're using an AUTO_INCREMENT column as the id, we can retrieve the new records id using *$wpdb->insert_id*.

A note about preparing SQL statements

It is good practice to prepare your SQL statements before running them on the database. This means escaping and validating any user inputted values. Wordpress provides this functionality via *$wpdb->prepare_ and should be called when using the generic query function, _$wpdb->query*. However, if you are using the specific query functions like *$wpdb->insert* and *$wpdb->update* you don't have to worry about preparing the statements as this is done for you by Wordpress.

```
function myplugin_update_record($id, $title, $desc, $isEnabled, $value)
{
    $data = array(
        'title' => $title,
        'desc' => $desc,
        'isEnabled' => $isEnabled,
        'value' => $value
    );

    global $wpdb;
    $rows_affected = $wpdb->update($wpdb->prefix . 'myplugin_table',
        $data, array('recordID' => $id));
    return $rows_affected;
}
```

The *$wpdb->update* function is similar to *$wpdb->insert* in that we pass it the table name and the data we wish to update. The final parameter is an array used as the WHERE clause in the SQL. In this case, we want to update the record with the id equal to *$id*.

```
function myplugin_delete_record($id)
{
    global $wpdb;
    $rows_affected = $wpdb->delete($wpdb->prefix . 'myplugin_table',
        array('recordID' => $id));
    return $rows_affected;
}
```

Deleting is similar in format to *$wpdb->update* except we don't pass data to update, just the WHERE clause as an array. In this case, we're instructing Wordpress to delete the record with the id equal to *$id* from our table.

```
function myplugin_get_all_records()
{
    global $wpdb;
    return $wpdb->get_results("SELECT * FROM " .
        $wpdb->prefix . "myplugin_table;");
}

function myplugin_get_record($id)
{
    global $wpdb;
    return $wpdb->get_row("SELECT * FROM " .
```

```
        $wpdb->prefix . "myplugin_table WHERE recordID=" . $id . ";");
}
```

The last two functions in our *include/my-plugin-database.php* file are for selecting data from the database table. To find out how many results are returned when calling $wpdb->get_results you can check *$wpdb->num_rows*. The results are returned as an array with each element an object representing a row. If you require just one row, *$wpdb->get_row* can be used and it returns an object representing the row as you can see in *myplugin_get_record*.

Here's an example of how you might use these new database functions in one of your admin menu pages:

```php
<?php
$records = myplugin_get_all_records();
?>


<div class="wrap">
    <h2><?php echo __('My Plugin Records', 'myplugin'); ?></h2>
    <table>
        <thead>
        <tr>
            <th>Title</th>
            <th>Description</th>
            <th>Is Enabled</th>
            <th>Value</th>
        </tr>
        </thead>
        <tbody>
        <?php foreach ($records as $row): ?>
        <tr>
            <td><?php echo $row->title; ?></td>
            <td><?php echo $row->desc; ?></td>
            <td><?php echo $row->isEnabled; ?></td>
            <td><?php echo $row->value; ?></td>
        </tr>
        <?php endforeach; ?>
        </tbody>
    </table>
</div>
```

Here we use our *myplugin_get_all_records* function to get everything from the table we created earlier. We then create a HTML table and loop around the results adding a new row for each database result row and echoing the values for each column.

Another example might be when we have an admin page containing a form, like the one we created in the earlier section on administrator menus, but instead of saving options we save a new record in the database. In this case, we'd simply follow all the same steps as before up to the handler function in *include/my-plugin-functions.php*. Then in the handler function we'd just call our new database function *myplugin_insert_record* with the values to store in the database.

Now we understand how to use the database through Wordpress, we can take a look at Shortcodes.

Shortcodes

Shortcodes allow your users to embed custom content into posts and pages. As a plugin developer, you create the shortcode, attach it to a function to handle the output of custom content, and then inform your users of the shortcode name. Wordpress has some shortcodes built in by default. For example, if a user created a new page and added the shortcode *[gallery]* as the content, Wordpress would interpret the shortcode and create a photo gallery on that page.

Shortcodes can also be passed attributes which you can use to customize their behavior. For example, the *[gallery]* shortcode may be customized by adding the "size" attribute: *[gallery size="medium"]*. The attribute is passed along to the handling code to be dealt with appropriately.

We will create a shortcode which can be used to create a form on any page or post they add the shortcode to. This form will be used to update entries in the database table we created in the previous section. In our main file *my-plugin.php* we'll add the following code:

```
add_shortcode('myplugin_form', 'myplugin_user_form');
function myplugin_user_form($atts)
{
    extract(shortcode_atts(array(
        'record' => -1,
    ), $atts));
    include 'pages/myplugin_user_form.php';
}
```

To register the shortcode with Wordpress we use *add_shortcode*. This takes the name of the shortcode as the first parameter and the name of the function to handle the shortcode as the second parameter. We've chosen "*myplugin_form*" as the name which means we want the shortcode to be *[myplugin_-form]*.

When Wordpress encounters our shortcode *[myplugin_form]* it will call *myplugin_user_form* passing any attributes that might have been added to the shortcode. Inside that function, we use *shortcode_atts* which takes an array of default values plus any attributes the user may have set. *shortcode_atts* will set any unset values to the defaults for you. We then use PHP *extract* which takes the resulting array and makes local variables named for the attribute keys. This is so we can more easily access the attribute values. Lastly, we include a page which will contain our form definition.

Next we'll create the file *pages/myplugin_user_form.php* which will contain the content we want to be displayed when the shortcode is added to a post or page.

```php
<?php
global $wpdb;
$valid = true;
$formData = $wpdb->get_row("SELECT * FROM " .
    $wpdb->prefix . "myplugin_table" . " WHERE recordID='" . $record . "';");

if ( !$formData ) {
    $valid = false;
    echo '<p class="alert alert-error">
            This form is invalid.
            Please check the settings and shortcode attributes</p>';
}
?>


<?php if ( $valid ): ?>
<form class="form-horizontal" action="" method="POST" id="user-form">
    <fieldset>
        <div id="legend">
            <legend class="">Edit Record
                <img src="<?php echo MY_PLUGIN_PATH . '/img/loader.gif'; ?>"
                    alt="Loading..." class="showLoading"/>
            </legend>
        </div>
        <input type="hidden" name="action" value="myplugin_update_record"/>
        <input type="hidden" name="recordID" value="<?php echo $record ?>"/>

        <p class="tips"></p>
        <label for="title"><?php _e("Title", 'myplugin'); ?> </label>
        <input type="text" name="title" id="title"
                value="<?php echo $formData->title; ?>">

        <label for="description"><?php _e("Description", 'myplugin'); ?>
        </label>
        <input type="text" name="description" id="description"
                value="<?php echo $formData->desc; ?>">

        <label for="value"><?php _e("Value", 'myplugin'); ?> </label>
        <input type="text" name="value" id="value"
                value="<?php echo $formData->value; ?>">

        <label><?php _e("Is Enabled", 'myplugin'); ?> </label>
        <label class="radio">
```

```
            <input type="radio" name="isEnabled" value="0"
                <?php echo ($formData->isEnabled == 0) ? 'checked' : '' ?> > No
        </label>
        <label class="radio">
            <input type="radio" name="isEnabled"  value="1"
                <?php echo ($formData->isEnabled == 1) ? 'checked' : '' ?>> Yes
        </label>

        <button type="submit" class="btn btn-success">
            <?php esc_attr_e('Save Changes') ?></button>


    </fieldset>
</form>
<?php endif; ?>
```

The first thing we do here is try to retrieve the record from the database with the id set by the user in the shortcode. Earlier, we made sure that if no id was set it would default to -1. If the id is invalid (which the default should be) then an error should appear on the post or page containing the shortcode, in place of where the form would be.

Following that is a straightforward form, similar to the form we used earlier for our administrator menu. This form will show the current values set for the record and allow the user to update those values. It also contains no action attribute in the form tag but instead a hidden field for the action with the value "*myplugin_update_record*". This is so we can use Ajax via Javascript to submit this form.

In order to enable Ajax from this shortcode form, we must first add a hook to make Wordpress include our Javascript file. Again, this is similar to how we did it in earlier for the administrator menus except now we're including the file on the user side not just for administrators. In *include/my-plugin-functions.php* we'll need to add the following:

```
add_action('wp_print_scripts', 'myplugin_load_js');
function myplugin_load_js()
{
    wp_enqueue_script('myplugin-user-js',
        MY_PLUGIN_PATH. '/js/myplugin.js', array('jquery'));
    wp_localize_script('myplugin-user-js',
        'ajaxurl', admin_url('admin-ajax.php'));
}
```

This will include a new file, *myplugin.js*, and make the variable *ajaxurl* available to it so it can post data back to the server. Our *myplugin.js* file will look like this:

```
jQuery(document).ready(function ($)
{
    $(".showLoading").hide();
    $('#user-form').submit(function (e)
    {
        $(".showLoading").show();
        $(".tips").removeClass('alert alert-error');
        $(".tips").html("");

        var $form = $(this);

        // Disable the submit button
        $form.find('button').prop('disabled', true);

        $.ajax({
            type:"POST",
            url:ajaxurl,
            data:$form.serialize(),
            cache:false,
            dataType:"json",
            success:function (data)
            {
                $(".showLoading").hide();
                // re-enable the submit button
                $form.find('button').prop('disabled', false);
                if (data.success)
                {
                    $(".tips").addClass('alert alert-error');
                    $(".tips").text("Settings updated");
                }
                else
                {
                    // show the errors on the form
                    $(".tips").addClass('alert alert-error');
                    $(".tips").html(data.msg);
                    $(".tips").fadeIn(500).fadeOut(500).fadeIn(500);
                }
            }
        });
        return false;
    });
});
```

You will notice how similar it is to *myplugin-admin.js* except here we don't have the "*updateMessage*" that administrators see and instead report back success or errors via a *<p>* on the form itself. The workings of this code have been explained earlier in the section on creating administrator menus. This code will execute when the user submits the form and will pass all the form data to the Wordpress *ajaxurl* via the jQuery *$.ajax* call. Because we defined an "action" of *myplugin_update_record* Wordpress will attempt to route this data to the correct function based on any hooks that have been registered with that name. Let's do that now in *include/my-plugin-functions.php*.

```php
add_action('wp_ajax_myplugin_update_record', 'myplugin_update_record');
add_action('wp_ajax_nopriv_myplugin_update_record', 'myplugin_update_record');
function myplugin_update_record()
{
    $id = $_POST['recordID'];
    $title = $_POST['title'];
    $desc= $_POST['description'];
    $value = $_POST['value'];
    $isEnabled = $_POST['isEnabled'];

    $rows_affected = myplugin_update_record($id, $title, $desc,
        $isEnabled, $value);
    $result = array('success' => true);
    if ($rows_affected === 0)
        $result = array('success' => false, 'msg' => 'Failed to update data');

    header("Content-Type: application/json");
    echo json_encode($result);
    exit;
}
```

Here we are adding Ajax hooks for both *wp_ajax* and *wp_ajax_nopriv* which means we want the action to work for users who are not logged in as well as for those who are. We then get the *$POST data from the form and use our database function _myplugin_update_record* to update the database row with the new values from the user. Bear in mind the note from the previous section regarding validating user input.While we don't include validation here, it is highly recommended that you validate any values passed from the user before passing them onto the database. Finally, we check if the update was successful and pass back the result to the Javascript which will display it to the user.

Now we have a working shortcode which will display a form that the user can use to edit a record from the database. All this is achieved with only two new functions in *include/my-plugin-functions.php*, a shortcode hook in *my-plugin.php* and the new page with its associated Javascript.

Next up, we'll take a quick look at how to include styles so we can alter the appearance of our pages.

Styling

That last step in completing our plugin is to style some of the pages we have created throughout the previous steps. Be careful when adding new styles so that they don't conflict or override any styles from other plugins or themes the user may have installed. Please note that the purpose of this section is not to create attractive forms but instead to show you the process of adding styles to your plugin pages.

We include new styles similar to including new scripts, using *wp_register_style* and *wp_enqueue_style*. You will remember earlier we registered and enqueued a style specifically for the administrator menus. Here's the relevant code from that section:

```
function myplugin_admin_init()
{
    wp_register_style('myplugin-css',
        MY_PLUGIN_PATH . '/css/myplugin-admin.css');
}


function myplugin_admin_scripts()
{
    wp_enqueue_style('myplugin-css');
}
```

This will ensure the CSS file *myplugin-admin.css* will be included on the administrator menu pages that are hooked in to load them. See the earlier section on creating administrator menus for full details of how we achieved this.

If we'd also like to include styles for user facing pages and posts (i.e. our shortcode update form created in earlier) we can hook into the *wp_print_styles* action, shown here in *include/my-plugin-functions.php*

```
add_action('wp_print_styles', 'myplugin_load_css');
function myplugin_load_css()
{
    wp_enqueue_style('myplugin-user-css', MY_PLUGIN_PATH . '/css/myplugin.css');
}
```

First, let's style the update record form we created in the section on Shortcodes. To give the form a nicer layout a simple first step is to wrap each label and its associated input inside a <p> tag. Here's an example of part of that process:

```
<p>
    <label for="title"><?php _e("Title", 'myplugin'); ?> </label>
    <input type="text" name="title" id="title"
        value="<?php echo $formData->title; ?>">
</p>
```

This should cause each label and input field to be displayed on separate lines. Now we want to tidy the fields up a bit so they are in line with one another. Create *css/myplugin.css* and add the following:

```
#user-form label
{
    text-align: right;
    float: left;
    width: 100px;
    padding-right: 20px;
}


#user-form input
{
    width: 200px;
    float: left;
}


#user-form fieldset p
{
    clear: both;
    padding: 15px;
}


#user-form legend
{
    font-size: 110%;
    font-weight: bold;
}
```

Notice how we're ensuring these CSS rules only affect our form with the id *user-form* to be sure we don't affect any other styles that may be active on the page. We also added some minor styling to the form legend to make it stand out a bit more.

We can provide similar styling to our administrator menu form created in earlier using the same CSS as above in *css/myplugin-admin.css* and changing *user-form* to *settings-form* in the code.

So there we have it, we now know how to include styles correctly for both our administrator menu pages and our user facing content as well. You can even include CSS frameworks like Bootstrap or Foundation by using the same techniques as shown above.

Code Complete

In the first section we learned all about the main plugin file and how Wordpress hooks work, as well as the correct way to include other files via our definition constants. Following that we learned all about creating administrator menus and how to create simple and top-level menus. We also introduced using Ajax for passing menu form input back to the server and how to handle that input. In the Databases section we created a database table during plugin activation and used *$wpdb* to access the table correctly. It was all about shortcodes next, with details on how to create custom shortcodes with attributes that output a form handled by Javascript. We finished up with a short description of adding styles so now you know how to properly include styles for individual pages or across your entire plugin.

If you followed the sections in order you should now have a working plugin containing all the major features. Of course, this example plugin doesn't do much so it's up to you to take your own idea and make a real plugin.

Good luck creating your own plugins and please share your creations with the community at creatingplugins.com[10]

---

[10]http://creatingplugins.com

Plugin Ideas

Now you know how to create a plugin, what are you going to make? Some people find coming up with ideas easy, while others struggle for weeks looking for that perfect idea. Here we'll discuss a few methods for generating ideas that have the best chance of selling.

When starting out with a new business, the number one rule is *"Make something people want"*. To make something people want we must first find out what it is they actually want. You can start your plugin idea research by grabbing a pen and notepad and going through the following steps:

- Asking friends and family about their day-to-day problems
- Speaking with local business owners about their operations
- Taking note of regular complaints from work colleagues
- Thinking about your own problems and annoyances

Most people are happy to talk about their problems and once you keep your mind open for ideas you'll find it becomes easier over time to spot a potential good one.

Obviously, you don't just have to stick to the real world when looking for ideas. The internet opens up your search to the entire world and you should certainly take advantage of it! Keeping your notepad on hand and your mind open for ideas, try the following:

- Browsing business forums looking for common complaints
- Join online communities and find out what they want by participating in the conversations
- Search for popular Wordpress plugins and think about how you could improve them
- Even better, find out what users of popular plugins would improve
- Search social media for problems people regularly bring up

By now, you should have quite a few ideas with some potential. You'll need to narrow down these ideas into a workable list of potential plugins. Try to rule out any that seem unrealistic or uninteresting first. Also, depending on your situation you may wish to rule out those that require a large budget up-front or those that will need a team of developers to complete. I recommend not ruling out ideas in what look like saturated markets right away. This is because even in markets with lots of providers there is usually room for more sellers, plus lots of companies in a market indicates it can be profitable.

Once you are down to only a few ideas, it's time to research the market to see if there are any potential buyers for your idea. You can do this by researching sellers of competing ideas on their websites, company records, marketplaces, news articles and so on. You can also get involved in the online communities related to your idea and find out what people are buying. If there are no competitors in your chosen idea "niche" it could indicate there is no money to be made there.

Hopefully you now have a great idea for a plugin and can now start working on creating it. In the following sections we'll discuss the various ways of selling your new Wordpress plugin.

Before Selling

Before you start selling your new plugin you must make sure it meets certain standards for the best chance of success. The first thing to do is to make sure there are no bugs or broken features in your code. Go through every action and test thoroughly making sure there are no errors, typos and that the UI is easy to understand. Turn on Wordpress debugging[11] and check that no errors or warnings are being outputted by your plugin code. Run through your plugin actions with the browser developer console open (F12 on Chrome, Ctrl+Shift+K on Firefox) and look for error messages, particularly from pages containing Javascript.

It's a good idea to get some test users first, usually friends or family. Let them use the plugin naturally with no input or advice from you. If you observe while they are using your plugin you can usually spot common issues they have and fix them before releasing it to the public.

When you are confident of the quality of your plugin you will then need to write documentation for it. The documentation should be written as if the user has never used Wordpress before, thoroughly explaining each part of your plugin (with images if necessary) in clear, well-written language. It is also useful to include a help page as an administrator menu item so that users can view help from within Wordpress itself. You can further improve the quality of your plugin by adding tool-tips and in-line help beside plugin areas such as settings forms and so on. If your plugin uses Shortcodes, see if you can generate them for your users so they can simply copy and paste when needed.

The small details are what make a good plugin into a great one. Great plugins sell much better and will also require less overhead on your part once released.

---

[11]http://codex.wordpress.org/Debugging_in_WordPress

Marketplaces

Online marketplaces are a great way to get started with selling your new plugin. They require very little work and cost on your part, plus the large ones boast millions of users all looking to spend money on plugins like yours.

The largest and most well known marketplace is CodeCanyon[12] which is part of the Envato network. CodeCanyon has nearly 3 million members at the time of writing. That's a lot of people looking to buy plugins and some of the top sellers have made over a million dollars in sales. While it is unrealistic to expect that kind of income early on, you can certainly make a good living selling plugins on marketplaces like CodeCanyon.

Getting started

Getting started with CodeCanyon (or most marketplaces) is quite straight-forward. There is a basic sign-up process and once signed up you can apply to become an author. Authors have the ability to add their products for sale on the marketplace. CodeCanyon does require authors to take an online test before being accepted. The test is a simple multiple choice and all the answers can be found by reading the CodeCanyon author tutorial.

Once you've passed the test to become an author you can start uploading your plugins for sale. For Wordpress plugins, you will need to zip the plugin into one main file plus provide screen-shots, a thumbnail image, a main sales image and a product description.

Create your main plugin file by navigating to the directory you have Wordpress installed, then *wp-content/plugins* and you will see your plugin directory (*my-plugin* if following the examples in earlier sections). Just right-click the directory and create a compressed zip file of the same name as your plugin i.e. *my-plugin.zip*.

For the screen-shots and thumbnail make sure you follow the author guidelines for the marketplace and use a tool such as Adobe Photoshop or GIMP to create the highest quality images possible. The product description can be written in HTML on CodeCanyon so use that to your advantage to make the description look professional.

Once you have all the files ready, follow the instructions on the marketplace for adding a new item and submit. CodeCanyon does have a review period for product submissions which can take up to 7 days although usually it is complete within 48 hours. If your product fails the review, don't worry! Just read the review comments carefully, make the suggested changes and try again.

If your plugin is accepted, CodeCanyon will pick a price based upon their own guidelines (quality, similar products pricing, etc.) and your plugin will be made available for purchase.

---

[12]http://codecanyon.net

Stand out from the crowd

Getting your plugin listed for sale is only the beginning. Sure, you may make a few sales early on but to make a good income you must stand out from the crowd. Luckily there are several ways you can help your plugin stand out from the crowd.

High quality presentation

You want your images and product description to capture peoples attention. Make sure your sales image contains the main benefits of your plugin clearly. Design your description so it explains exactly how your plugin will solve it's buyers problems. Ensure you list all the features of your plugin in a way that speaks to the issues your market/niche has and how the feature solves those issues. If your plugin can save or earn money for its users, tell them exactly how much in the description.

Your product screen-shots should be of the highest quality you can make and should accurately show all parts of your plugin. If you don't provide a demo (see below) then the screen-shots are the most important part after the description.

Finally, you want to make sure your user profile page is of a high quality. It should tell people all about you and your skills and why they should buy from you.

Product demo and video

Providing a live demo of your plugin is a great way of increasing sales. Potential buyers get to see all the features and the quality of your plugin for themselves. Providing an in-depth product video is also worthwhile as many users prefer to be led through all the features this way.

Creating a live demo doesn't have to be difficult or costly. There are many free and cheap hosting solutions out there on which you can run a basic version of Wordpress. Just install your plugin and create a demo user login for potential buyers. It is recommended you try to lock down permissions on these demo users via the Wordpress Users administrator menu. It's also wise to reset the website on occasion.

There is plenty of free software available for creating product videos, in particular called screencasts. Screencasts will record what is on your screen (and your voice if you wish) so you can walk potential buyers through your plugin while explaining each part and its benefits.

Customer support

Offering great customer support is a sure way to increase your sales. Users who receive great support will tell others about it either directly or indirectly in the form of ratings and reviews.

Most users on marketplaces have little technical understanding and are just looking for a product to solve a particular need or problem they have. It is important when dealing with these users that you always remain calm and polite. You must take time to formulate detailed, non-technical responses to their questions and always be perceived as open and happy to help.

The faster you can respond to user comments or questions the better. Sites like CodeCanyon show the time of comments and responses so other users will see how fast you respond and will be impressed making them more likely to buy.

Make an effort to browse the forums (most marketplaces have them) and help people out, even helping people in no way related to purchasing your plugin. As you become well-known for being knowledgeable and helping others more people will take the time to look at your profile and products.

Regular updates

One thing people love is getting more for their money. Make sure to regularly update your plugin with improvements and new features.

Your plugin updates need not be large undertakings. Simple improvements to the UI, more help pages or even minor new features are all worth doing. Each time you do an update make sure to list the details of the update in the product description so potential buyers can see. If potential buyers see a long, regularly updated list of changes they will feel confident that your plugin is a quality product that gives them a lot of value for their money.

Downsides to marketplaces

The biggest downside to using a marketplace to sell your plugin is the revenue split. CodeCanyon takes 50% of every sale for new authors, down to 30% after you've made several thousand sales. With the average price of plugins on CodeCanyon selling between $20-$50 you can see it will take a lot of sales to earn a decent living. For their 50%, CodeCanyon has millions of potential buyers visiting the website regularly, plus they handle all the file storage and billing so you don't have to worry about it. CodeCanyon also picks the selling price of your plugin which can be limiting as well.

The other major downside of using a marketplace is the type of buyer it attracts. It is quite a well known phenomenon that buyers focused solely on cheapest price often cause the most headaches in terms of support, questions, refunds and so on. While most buyers are fine, you will find a good percentage of buyers expect too much for their money. For a $20 plugin (of which you receive $10) some buyers will expect you to help them install the plugin, make customizations and other support all for free. These buyers are often the same ones who give bad reviews and ratings if you don't comply so a lot of marketplace authors feel compelled to do so. It is a fine line to tread and something to be aware of when starting out on a new marketplace.

It's up to you to decide if the downsides are worth it. For a first time seller, I'd highly recommend using a marketplace like CodeCanyon to learn what it takes to be successful at selling plugins. Once you have a good handle on how everything works, you might start thinking that you can make more money doing some of it yourself. This is where creating your own website comes in.

Plugin Website

Creating a website to promote your plugins is a smart thing to do. Not only is it extra marketing for your work, but a well designed website will add to your image and professionalism.

Getting Started

You don't need to spend a lot of time or money on your website. With tools like Wordpress you can put together a professional looking website in no time. There are numerous free plugins online which can add all the features you need for your website.

First though, you'll need to purchase a domain name and some web hosting. There's a good chance you already know how to do this (readers of this book are already quite technical) but for those who don't the steps are simple. Pick a domain that is related to your plugins in some way, isn't too long, is easy to spell and is preferably a .com domain and head to a registrar (like Namecheap[13]) to purchase. Hosting can be free if you use a service like Wordpress or Tumblr[14] or relatively cheap on shared hosting plans from the likes of GoDaddy[15] and JustHost[16]. If you're planning on a lot of traffic or running several websites and know a bit about managing servers then a VPS from Linode[17] or DigitalOcean[18] might be suitable.

Installing Wordpress on your hosting is similar to installing it locally which was explained at the beginning of the book.

Essentials

Now you have a new website setup on your hosting, it's time to get the essentials added. Obviously you'll need pages to describe your plugins. Make sure these pages detail exactly how the plugins solve potential buyers problems or how they can make/save them money because these are the things people care about. You should also include a list of all the features, your list of updates and several high quality images of the plugins pages. A live demo and a video of the product in use are also recommended. While you are still selling your plugins via the marketplace you will want your website plugin pages to direct people to the marketplace to make the purchase. Don't forget to take advantage of any marketplace affiliate/referral schemes here too. Usually this just involves

[13]http://namecheap.com
[14]http://tumblr.com
[15]http://godaddy.com
[16]http://justhost.com
[17]http://linode.com
[18]http://digitalocean.com

appending your affiliate/referral ID to the end of the URL and you can make a few more dollars per sale.

Next you'll want to provide an "about" page. Buyers want to know who they are paying. They'd also like to know your credentials and what makes you a good person to buy from. Adding a picture of yourself is also recommended because people like to know they are doing business with a real person.

You also need to provide buyers a way to contact you. Most of the time this is an email address but you can also provide a contact form or even a support forum on your website. If you are selling high-end plugins ($200+ price) I recommend adding a phone number as well. People who are likely to spend more than $200 often want to ask a few questions on the phone first.

Selling from your website

The website is built and attracting visitors but you're not happy redirecting the visitors to the marketplace to sell your plugins for a 50% cut. With the number of visitors you receive you could make far more selling directly from your website. It's time to move away from the marketplace and get your website setup for direct sales.

Digital sales hosting

One method of selling your products from your website is to use a third-party service like GumRoad[19]. GumRoad will take care of all the payment transactions and hosting costs of storing your plugin files for only 5%. The 5% cut is a far better deal then the 50% that CodeCanyon or other marketplaces take. Using GumRoad (or similar services) means you don't have to worry about security when handling payments, or paying for hosting all your files either. All you have to do is add the simple code GumRoad provides and your customers can buy directly from your website securely. GumRoad will send your customers the files automatically and will pay you directly to your bank account.

Selling directly

If you're prefer complete control you can accept credit cards on your website and handle the storage of your plugin files too. To accept credit cards you will need an account with a payment gateway provider like Stripe[20], Authorize.Net[21] or Braintree[22]. These providers manage the credit card processing for a 2.9% fee. They will require some coding integration on your part however there are plenty of plugins online which can do this for you if you are running a Wordpress site.

---

[19] http://gumroad.com

[20] https://stripe.com

[21] http://www.authorize.net/

[22] https://www.braintreepayments.com/

WP Full Stripe[23] is a good example of a plugin which allows you to take payments using Stripe. Be aware that if you want to accept credit cards from your website you will need an SSL certificate for extra security. These can be found for a reasonable price at places like Namecheap and GoDaddy.

You also need to consider online storage for your plugins if you want to automatically deliver to your customers after purchase. You can use a service like Dropbox[24] or Amazon S3[25] and there are plugins which help you manage those as well.

---

[23]http://mammothology.com/products/view/wp-full-stripe

[24]http://dropbox.com

[25]http://aws.amazon.com/s3/

Social Selling

One of the key ways to improve your sales is to get your plugins in front of more people who are interested in purchasing them. This is where online communities and deal websites come in.

Deals

Deal websites like Mighty Deals[26] and AppSumo[27] are full of short-term special offers and promotions. Mighty Deals is focused on web designers and developers which can be a good fit depending on the type of plugin you are selling. Most deal sites expect you to offer your plugin at a heavy discount but they can provide so many sales that you make up for it in volume. The other benefit of using deal sites is the extra exposure. If you have several plugins for sale and list one of them on a deal site it is very likely sales of your other full price plugins will increase as well.

Facebook and Twitter

Building up a strong, targeted following on social media websites like Facebook and Twitter can be a full time job. However, when done correctly, every tweet or post you send out can lead to sales. The key to success on Facebook and Twitter is to provide regular, valuable content to your followers. Also, make sure to interact with people on the platform and reciprocate when people like or re-tweet your content. For the best results you should be posting new content several times a day. Services like Buffer[28] or HootSuite[29] can help with this.

Mailing list

A mailing list full of potential buyers can be a gold mine of sales if used correctly. You should ask for your buyers and website visitors email address whenever you can. Usually it is a good idea to offer something in return for joining your mailing list, perhaps a free plugin or article. Adding past buyers to your mailing list means you have a list of people you know will spend money on what you are selling. With that in mind, every email you send out to the list which promotes your plugins has a high potential of making sales. You can use free services like MailChimp[30] and SendGrid[31] to manage your mailing lists for you.

---

[26]http://www.mightydeals.com/
[27]http://www.appsumo.com
[28]http://bufferapp.com/
[29]http://hootsuite.com/
[30]http://mailchimp.com
[31]http://sendgrid.com

Guest posts

Guest posts on popular blogs are a great way of building exposure and increasing your perceived expertise - both of which lead to more sales. One of the hardest parts of guest posting is finding suitable blogs to post on. You can search Google to find blogs that are related to your plugins using commands like so:

```
inpostauthor:guest [your niche]
inurl:category/guest [your niche]
```

For example, if you have a plugin helps with SEO, you might search Google for inpostauthor:guest SEO which would return a list of blogs that accept guest posts for the topic of SEO.

Make sure your guest blog posts are relevant, well written and fit the blogs guidelines and you are more likely to be accepted. Also make sure you are on hand to answer any comments when the post is published.

Putting It All Together

The best way of increasing sales is to use all the methods we've described together. When you start out selling your plugins on the marketplace it's a good idea to also have a website because marketplace users like to research plugin authors and often look for a website. When first moving from marketplace sales to selling from your website, it makes sense to do this gradually by only moving one or two of your plugins at a time. This way you can direct marketplace users to your website in your plugin descriptions and therefore take advantage of all the traffic marketplaces receive.

Running ads and deals can be done at the same time to increase sales and visitors to your website. Posting on blogs and forums can be done all the time as well. You should post testimonials and good ratings to your marketplace product descriptions and your website as soon as you receive them. The key is a well rounded strategy to make sure as many people as possible know about your plugins.

A high amount of sales comes from a large number of targeted users being directed to your products combined with a professional image, high quality plugins, top customer support and good ratings from past buyers.

Good luck with selling your plugins! Please feel free to share your plugins with us at http://creatingplugins.com[32]

---

[32]http://creatingplugins.com

Where to find more information

You will find the sample code for this book here: https://github.com/josborne/creating-wordpress-plugins-sample-code[33]

Wordpress Plugin Basics: http://codex.wordpress.org/Writing_a_Plugin[34]

Wordpress Data Validation: http://codex.wordpress.org/Data_Validation[35]

Wordpress Plugin API: http://codex.wordpress.org/Plugin_API[36]

Wordpress Shortcode API: http://codex.wordpress.org/Shortcode_API[37]

The Wordpress $wpdb function reference: http://codex.wordpress.org/Class_Reference/wpdb[38]

Online community all about plugins: http://creatingplugins.com[39]

Marketplace: CodeCanyon[40]

Deals websites: Mighty Deals[41] and AppSumo[42]

Payment Processors: Stripe[43], Authorize.Net[44] and Braintree[45].

---

[33] https://github.com/josborne/creating-wordpress-plugins-sample-code
[34] http://codex.wordpress.org/Writing_a_Plugin
[35] http://codex.wordpress.org/Data_Validation
[36] http://codex.wordpress.org/Plugin_API
[37] http://codex.wordpress.org/Shortcode_API
[38] http://codex.wordpress.org/Class_Reference/wpdb
[39] http://creatingplugins.com
[40] http://codecanyon.net
[41] http://www.mightydeals.com/
[42] http://www.appsumo.com
[43] https://stripe.com
[44] http://www.authorize.net/
[45] https://www.braintreepayments.com/

www.ingramcontent.com/pod-product-compliance
Lightning Source LLC
Chambersburg PA
CBHW060509060326
40689CB00020B/4686